THIS BOOK BELONGS TO

_____

Enjoy
Sarah Boudreau

Enjoy the colors of the "Granite State" all year long!
✗ Angela Welch ✗

THE COLORS OF NEW HAMPSHIRE
Copyright © 2021 by Angela Welch

ISBN 13: 978-1-7368216-1-9
Library of Congress PCN: 2021913526

All Rights Reserved. No parts of this book may be reproduced or utilized in any form or by any means, electronic or mechanical, including photocopying, scanning, recording, or by any information storage and retrieval system now known or hereafter invented, without permission, in writing from the publisher.

To order a copy of this book, please visit
www.amitypublications.com.

Design and Layout by
AMITY Publications
www.amitypublications.com

Printed in the United States of America

THE COLORS OF NEW HAMPSHIRE

Written By Angela Welch

Illustrated by Sarah Boudreau

New Hampshire is a kaleidoscope of color all year through.

The summer brings greens of mountains and a sky of blue.

The fall brings browns, oranges, yellows and bright red.

Then winter brings the snow blanketing all white instead.

The spring brings new flowers with all colors everywhere.

People also leave their color designs with their own flair.

Colorful lights are seen at town fairs or an amusement park.

The fireworks shot in the summer sky weekly after dark.

The painted carousel horses children ride, up and down.

The lights of outdoor restaurants all over cities and towns.

The skiers and snowboarders swish back and forth fast.

Children run at recess and wonder if the fun will last.

Colorful kites at the beach weave and dip in the breeze.

The colorful flowers in the garden can make you sneeze.

The colors of the lights are a sight at a large fall fair.

The colors of New Hampshire can be found everywhere.

The color of New Hampshire is RED like the...

Streams of ribbons from the tail lights on the highways.

Bricks of the old mill buildings made of rust color clay.

Covered bridges over rivers with only one lane.

Cardinals darting in and out of trees to avoid the rain.

Maple leaves of fall in all their scarlet glory.

Chipped paint on the side of the old ruddy dory.

Sturdy barns standing tall keeping all dry within.

Tugboats on the Piscataqua bringing the ships in.

The color of New Hampshire is **RED**.

The color of New Hampshire is **GREEN** like the...

Tree covered mountains rising up from the valleys.

Shaded vacation campsites made for many families.

Speckled bull frogs croaking near the marshes and streams.

Luna moth gently flapping its wings as if in a dream.

Grasshoppers jumping in a field on a hot July afternoon.

Tall fields of sweet corn to be picked very soon.

Statues in parks that honor people in our past.

Reminders to recycle so our state will forever last.

The color of New Hampshire is **GREEN**.

The color of New Hampshire is **BLUE** like the...

Clear and flawless cobalt sky on a cloudless sunny day.

Wings of a beautiful screeching blue jay.

Lake Winnipesaukee from Mount Major's mountain top.

Mighty Merrimack River flowing south non-stop.

New Hampshire flag with a background of a dark hue.

Quiet paddling on a still pond in a shiny new canoe.

Cornflowers and bluebells growing in fields of grass.

Bits of frosted sparkle in the tide pools known as sea glass.

The color of New Hampshire is BLUE.

The color of New Hampshire is **YELLOW** like the...

Sunflowers standing tall in the fields of farms of Lee.

Lobster boat in Rye Harbor sailing out to sea.

Goldfinch with its golden wings warbling in the trees.

Leaves of the birch trees fluttering in the breeze.

Spotted salamander that can live in water and on land.

Pail and shovel of a child laying in the Hampton Beach sand.

Smiling hot air balloon over Salem as it huffs and puffs on by.

Train station in North Conway or a sunrise over the ocean in Rye.

The color of New Hampshire is **YELLOW**.

The color of New Hampshire is PURPLE like the...

State bird, the Purple Finch, that really isn't purple at all.

Notched-mouth Ground Beetle, very dark and not small.

Ripening blueberries growing everywhere across the state.

Boxcar on a fast train in Exeter pulling a lot of freight.

Beautiful Lupines that grow in the town of Sugar Hill.

Fancy violet ski suits at Gunstock moving fast with expert skill.

State flower, the Purple Lilac, in colors dark or light.

Color of the sky at twilight before day slowly turns to night.

The color of New Hampshire is PURPLE.

The color of New Hampshire is **ORANGE** like the...

Sun setting over Lake Chocorua casting an auburn glow.

Pumpkin patches in October waiting for people to show.

Town of Orange named for its ochre-colored clay.

Beautiful Tiger lilies that bloom on a hot summer day.

Flickering lights of jack-o-'lanterns at Keene's festival.

Paper tickets bought for rides at a weekend carnival.

Monarch butterfly wings looking like tangerine-stained glass.

State's amphibian, the red-spotted newt, lying in wet grass.

The color of New Hampshire is **ORANGE**.

The color of New Hampshire is BROWN like the...

Color of the porcupines with their sharp and pointed quills.

Acorns falling from oak trees yet the leaves hang on still.

Wood that built Charlestown's Old Fort at Number Four.

Stink Bug that tries to visit through your window or door.

Horseshoe crabs to be found in and around the Great Bay.

Chocolate ice cream in a cone to eat on a hot summer day.

Color of the majestic moose as it moves about the brush.

Herds of leaping white-tailed deer, always in a rush.

The color of New Hampshire is **BROWN**.

The color of New Hampshire is **BLACK** like the...

Old Peppersass, the first engine of the old Cog Railway.

Great big bears that slowly cross the Kancamagus Scenic Biway.

Delicate head of a loon as it floats along in Squam Lake.

Eastern Timber Rattler, our most endangered viper snake.

Dark and cool wide mouthed caverns of the many Polar Caves.

Quiet skunk moving slowly along before it misbehaves.

Dark shadows of clouds crossing the mountains overhead.

Swarming flies of spring whose arrival is viewed with dread.

The color of New Hampshire is **BLACK**.

The color of New Hampshire is **GRAY** like the...

Top of Mount Monadnock standing tall on our western land.

State House built of granite that will forever stand.

Famous submarine Albacore at a Portsmouth park for all to see.

Revere Bell ringing every hour in a Hancock church belfry.

Granite face of Franconia's Old Man who is now forever gone.

Elephant Head of Crawford Notch always facing a new dawn.

Boulders piled at the bottom of the Amoskeag waterfall.

Fisher Cat logo for the Manchester team that plays baseball.

The color of New Hampshire is **GRAY**.

The color of New Hampshire is **WHITE** like the...

Top of Mount Washington's frozen snowcapped peak in winter.

Paper-like bark of the White Birch that peels but doesn't splinter.

Buildings of the Isles of Shoals, so bright from afar in the sun.

Snowdrops peeking up from the ground when the winter season is done.

Beautiful old grand hotels in the mountains or by the sea.

Graceful Snowy Owl as it flies slowly to perch on a tree.

Flashing lighthouse at Portsmouth guiding all ships in the same.

Town called Whitefield, not for color, just part of its name.

The color of New Hampshire is **WHITE**.

It's been fun thinking about the colors and we're done too soon.
Derry astronaut Alan Shepard's white spacesuit went to the moon.
Crawford Notch has the Frankenstein Trestle painted all black.
Lincoln has The Flume Gorge, formed by an ancient 800-foot crack.

Whenever you are in New Hampshire, please take a look.
What colors do you notice that are included in this book?
What are the things and the places you are able to see
That makes our State of New Hampshire the best place to be!

Discover the Colors of New Hampshire for Yourselves.

RED
Covered Bridges: www.visitwhitemountains.com
Belknap Mill Museum, Laconia: www.belknapmill.org

GREEN
White Mountains: www.visitwhitemountains.com
General Stark Statue at Stark Park-Manchester, NH: www.starkpark.com
Millie the Mill Girl at the Millyard Museum: www.manchesterhistoric.org

BLUE
Lake Winnipesaukee Area: www.lakesregion.org
Sea Glass Hunting: www.odysseyseaglass.com

YELLOW
Balloon Rides: www.high5ballooning.com
www.balloonridesnh.com
North Conway Train Station: www.conwayscenic.com

PURPLE
Sugar Hill Lupines: www.onlyinyourstate.com
www.franconianotch.org
Blueberry picking: www.pickyourown.org/NH

ORANGE
Pumpkin Festival, Keene: www.pumpkinfestival.org
Town of Orange: www.nhfamilyhikes.com/hikes
www.nhstateparks.org/visit

BROWN
Fort At No.4 - Charlestown, NH: www.fortat4.org
Horseshoe Crabs: The Great Bay National Estuarine Research Reserve
Greenland: www.greatbay.org

BLACK
The Mount Washington Cog Railway: www.thecog.com
The Polar Caves Rumney, NH: www.polarcaves.com

GRAY
The USS Albacore Museum, Portsmouth: www.ussalbacore.org
Mount Monadnock State Park, Jaffrey: www.nhstateparks.org/visit

WHITE
Isles of Shoals-Star Island: www.starisland.org
McAuliffe-Shepard Discovery Center, Concord: www.starhop.com

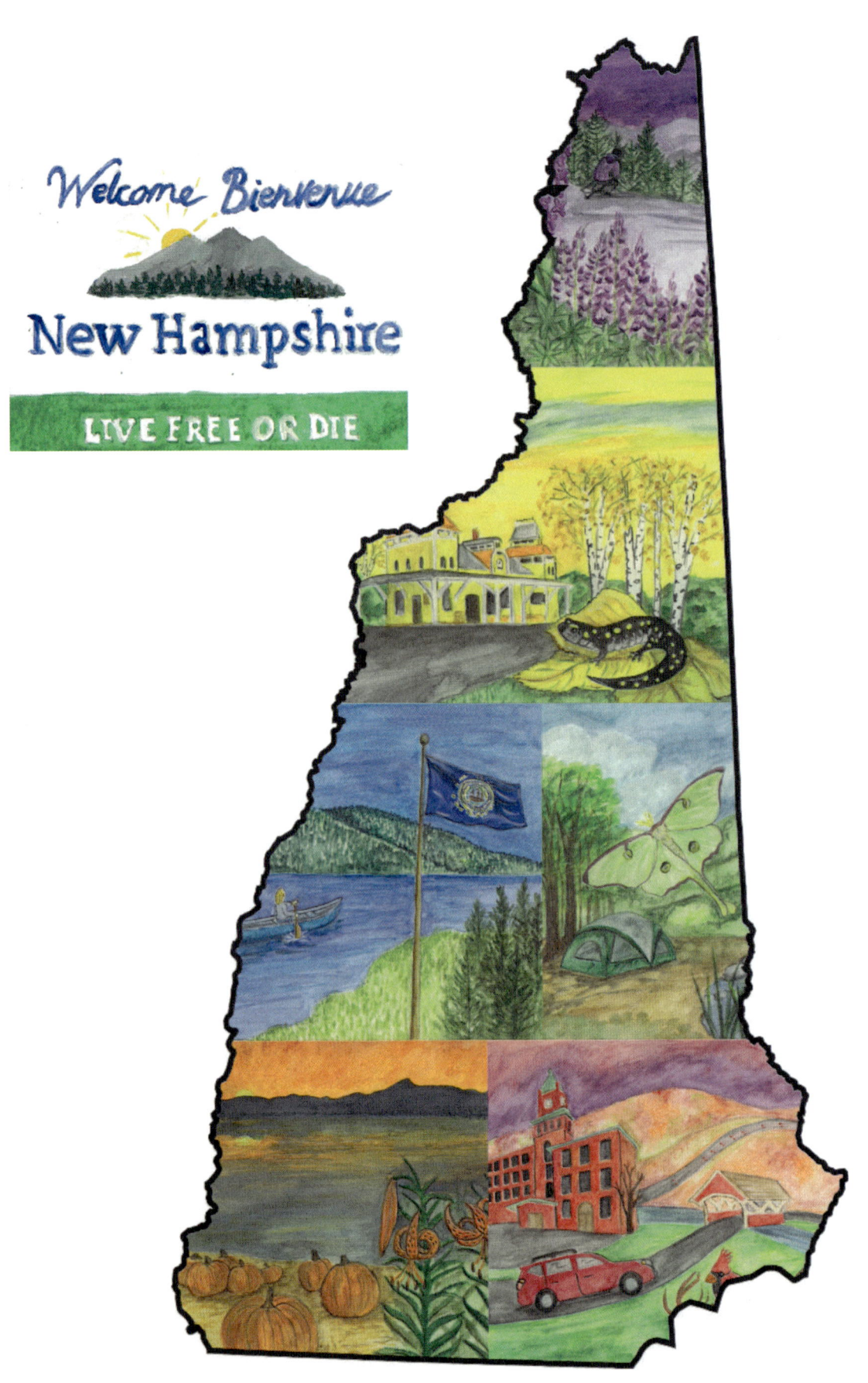

Made in the USA
Middletown, DE
06 April 2023